FREIGHT DISPATCHING FOR BEGINNERS

Freight Dispatching For Beginners

ALICE BEVERLY

Purposefully Write Publishing, LLC

Copyright © 2022 by Alice Beverly

All rights reserved. No part of this book may be reproduced in any manner whatsoever without written permission except in the case of brief quotations embodied in critical articles and reviews.

First Printing, 2022

Contents

INTRODUCTION	1
WHAT IS A DISPATCHER?	2
GETTING STARTED	3
DOCUMENTS YOU NEED TO SETUP A CARRIER	6
HOW DO I FIND A TRUCK TO DISPATCH?	8
DISPATCHER DUTIES OVERVIEW	15
EQUIPMENT TYPES	17
HOW MUCH SHOULD YOUR TRUCK MAKE?	22
LOAD BOARD NAVIGATION	24
SETTING RATES	28
BOOKING A LOAD	33
REQUESTING A CERTIFICATE OF INSURANCE	40
COMPLETING A CARRIER SETUP PACKET	43
DISPATCHING YOUR TRUCK	59
PROCESSING PAPERWORK FOR PAYMENT	61
PAYMENT STATUS CHECK	64
HOW TO FILE A CLAIM AGAINST A BOND	65
SAMPLE DISPATCHING SCRIPT	69
TRUCKING GLOSSARY	70

INTRODUCTION

I began in the freight industry working alongside my husband in his trucking business. This guide is useful for newbies, independent motor carriers who want to dispatch their own truck, or anyone wanting to create an additional stream of income. Take a few moments to read through this information in its entirety and let's get moving!

WHAT IS A DISPATCHER?

A dispatcher is a person who works with a licensed and/or bonded independent motor carrier as an employee of the motor carrier, or as an independent contractor. A dispatcher *IS NOT* a broker which is something totally different. The licensed motor carrier gives the dispatcher permission to negotiate freight rates, complete carrier setup packets, and submit invoices for payment on behalf of the carrier for a fee. The dispatcher acts as a liaison between the motor carrier and broker.

Scenario: Frank is an Independent Carrier at Speedy Express Trucking. He owns a 53 foot dry van trailer. He needs a dispatcher to make phone calls to different companies. Frank feels he could be getting better rates if he worked with a dispatcher. He would like to use someone that has experience in the trucking industry, communicates well and is detail oriented. Anna's Dispatching Service reaches out to him to tell him about the service she offers. They talk about the equipment he has and the lanes he likes to travel and the lanes he tries to avoid. Frank explains to Anna's Dispatching Service what his dollar per mile rate is in order to make a profit. Anna sends Speedy Express Trucking her dispatching contract that outlines her duties and her fee, and also her Tax ID number and payment information, as well as the documents she will need from Speedy Express Trucking. Speedy Express Trucking reads over the contract and decides he would like to use her services. He signs the contract and submits the necessary paperwork to get started with Anna. Anna's Dispatching Service can now dispatch on behalf of Speedy Express Trucking.

GETTING STARTED

1. A reliable computer with internet access to a load board

2. Notebook - to write down notes about loads you call on

3. Cheat Sheet- to record the drivers info like company name, MC#, DOT#, EIN#, Driver Phone number, Truck and Trailer Number, and address- you can take this information with you on the go.

4. Pens/Pencils

5. Calculator- to calculate rates, mileage, and fuel

6. Email address for dispatching only- you can create a simple Gmail email address to receive rate confirmations and new carrier

7. Calendar- to keep track of scheduled pick-up and delivery appointments for motor carriers and payment schedules

8. Smart Phone-use apps that are compatible with your smartphone

    - Adobe fill and Sign- download app on phone
    - Camera Scanner app- download on desktop/laptop
    - Jpeg to PDF converter app- download on desktop/laptop
    - PDF merge-download on desktop/laptop
    - Fuel book app

Adobe Fill and Sign App

This free app allows you to fill out and sign PDF versions of rate confirmations, carrier packets, W9's, etc. I download this app to my smart phone and am able to work while I am on the go.

JPEG to PDF

This free app converts jpeg files into PDF documents. Your motor carrier should not send you jpegs of documents they have taken with their phone. But if the pictures are clear, you can use this app to convert it into a PDF document.

Camera Scanner

This free app converts paperwork such as BOL's into PDF documents. The app uses your phone's camera to scan images into PDF documents.

PDF Merger

This free app allows you to combine all your PDF documents. I use this app to combine the carrier contract, operating authority, certificate of insurance, W-9, Notice of Assignment, and other documents to send as one file to the broker. I also use this app to combine carrier **invoices**, rate confirmations, BOL's, and any accessorial charges like lumper receipts.

Fuel App

This free app allows you to set the origin and destination so you can view the fuel prices along the trucking route. (i.e. Atlanta GA, Asheboro NC)

DOCUMENTS YOU NEED TO SETUP A CARRIER

When a motor carrier decides to use your dispatching service, the following documents are what you will need to get started. You will need PDF versions of these documents. Do not begin dispatching for a truck until you receive all the documents you need.

Step 1: Create a folder on your desktop/and or laptop and label it the motor carrier's company.

Speedy Express Trucking

Step 2: Download the motor carrier's PDF documents into your folder. You should have the following:

1. Operating Authority
2. Certificate of Insurance W-9
3. Notice of Assignment (if the motor carrier has a factoring company)
4. Voided business check with company name and address (no starter checks)
5. Driver's license photo (some brokers require this)

Step 3: Create an information sheet with the following information to take with you on the go:

1. Company information (address, phone #, EIN#)
2. Truck # and year

3. Trailer # and year
4. Last 6 number of tractor Vin # (some brokers require this)
5. Truck miles/gallon (optional)

Step 4: Now you can begin dispatching for your Motor Carrier.

HOW DO I FIND A TRUCK TO DISPATCH?

Word of mouth is by far the most cost effective and easiest way to begin freight dispatching. If you have family members or friends who have their own authority and trucks of their own, you can tell them about the services you provide. Explain what equipment you work with, and how you can help them negotiate competitive rates for their truck, complete carrier setup packets, and assist with the day to day operation as it pertains to dispatching the truck. Social media is another great way to promote your services. The FMCSA publishes authorities. You can google "fmcsa carrier search". Click on "Licensing & Insurance Carrier Search-Transportation".

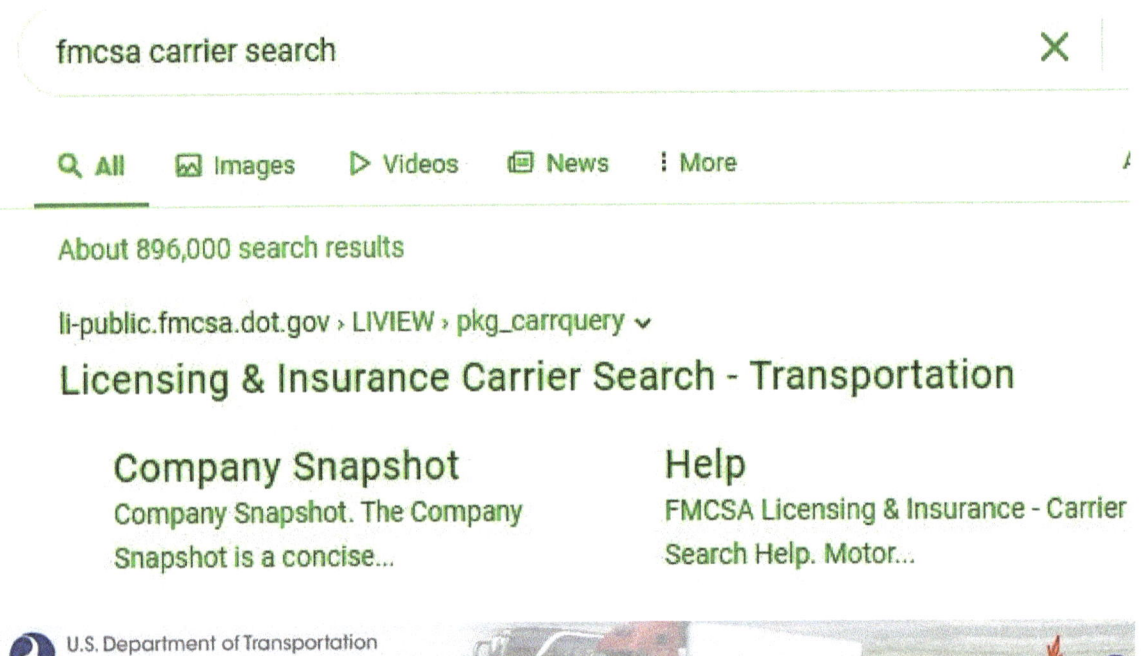

Select "FMCSA Carrier" from the drop-down menu at the top right corner and select go. Click on the html version of the document and scroll to the section titled "Certificate, Permit, License". I want to make it clear that NOT ALL the authorities published are ACTIVE and you will have to check it through the safer website by entering the MC or DOT#.

FREIGHT DISPATCHING

Motor Carrier Information Sheet

Motor Carrier Name:_____ Length of Authority:_____
MC#_____ DOT#_____
- ☐ Sole Prop/Single Member LLC
- ☐ C corp
- ☐ S corp
- ☐ Partnership

Address:_____
EIN #:_____Truck #_____Truck Year:_____
Last 6 of Vin#_____Trailer #_____ Trailer Year:_____
Miles per gallon:_____ max weight:_____

Insurance

Insurance Agent Name:_____Agent email:_____
Phone #_____ Fax #_____
Expires:_____

Username:
Password:

Username:
Password:

Username:
Password:

Authority

U.S. Department of Transportation
Federal Motor Carrier Safety Administration

1200 New Jersey Ave., S.E.
Washington, DC 20590

SERVICE DATE

DECISION

MC-

D/B/A

REENTITLED

On _____ applicant filed a request to have the Federal Motor Carrier Safety Administration's records changed to reflect a name change.

Presently, this applicant has no active authority on file with the Federal Motor Carrier Safety Administration. For purposes of changing the FMCSA's records, this name change will be processed.

It is ordered:

The Federal Motor Carrier Safety Administration's records are amended to reflect the carrier's name as _____

The applicant must establish that it is in full compliance with the statute and the insurance regulations by having amended filings on prescribed FMCSA forms (BMC91 or 91X or 82 for bodily injury and property damage liability, BMC 34 or 83 for cargo liability, or a BMC 84 or 85 for broker security and BOC-3 for designation of agents upon whom process may be served) submitted on its behalf. Copies of Form MCS-90 or other "certificates of insurance" are not acceptable evidence of insurance compliance. Insurance and BOC-3 filings should be sent to Federal Motor Carrier Safety Administration, 1200 New Jersey Ave., S.E., Washington, DC 20590.

If the applicant's authority has been revoked, it may submit a written request for reinstatement to the Federal Motor Carrier Safety Administration, P.O. BOX 530226, Atlanta, GA 30353-0226, (express/overnight delivery address is Bank of America, Lockbox Number 530226, 1075 Loop Road, Atlanta, GA 30337), accompanied by a filing fee of $80, in addition to submitting appropriate insurance filings on the prescribed FMCSA forms. If a motor carrier has an unsatisfactory safety rating, its authority registration will not be reinstated, and it should contact the nearest FMCSA Division Office to arrange for a review of its safety compliance prior to seeking reinstatement.

Decided: _____
By the Federal Motor Carrier Safety Administration

Jeffrey L. Secrist, Chief
Information Technology Operations Division

NCJ

Example

CERTIFICATE OF LIABILITY INSURANCE

DATE (MM/DD/YYYY)

THIS CERTIFICATE IS ISSUED AS A MATTER OF INFORMATION ONLY AND CONFERS NO RIGHTS UPON THE CERTIFICATE HOLDER. THIS CERTIFICATE DOES NOT AFFIRMATIVELY OR NEGATIVELY AMEND, EXTEND OR ALTER THE COVERAGE AFFORDED BY THE POLICIES BELOW. THIS CERTIFICATE OF INSURANCE DOES NOT CONSTITUTE A CONTRACT BETWEEN THE ISSUING INSURER(S), AUTHORIZED REPRESENTATIVE OR PRODUCER, AND THE CERTIFICATE HOLDER.

IMPORTANT: If the certificate holder is an ADDITIONAL INSURED, the policy(ies) must have ADDITIONAL INSURED provisions or be endorsed. If SUBROGATION IS WAIVED, subject to the terms and conditions of the policy, certain policies may require an endorsement. A statement on this certificate does not confer rights to the certificate holder in lieu of such endorsement(s).

PRODUCER: Insurance Company information

CONTACT NAME:
PHONE (A/C, No, Ext):
FAX (A/C, No):
E-MAIL ADDRESS:

INSURER(S) AFFORDING COVERAGE | **NAIC #**
INSURER A :
INSURER B :
INSURER C :
INSURER D :
INSURER E :
INSURER F :

INSURED: Motor Carrier's information

COVERAGES   CERTIFICATE NUMBER: REVISION NUMBER:

THIS IS TO CERTIFY THAT THE POLICIES OF INSURANCE LISTED BELOW HAVE BEEN ISSUED TO THE INSURED NAMED ABOVE FOR THE POLICY PERIOD INDICATED. NOTWITHSTANDING ANY REQUIREMENT, TERM OR CONDITION OF ANY CONTRACT OR OTHER DOCUMENT WITH RESPECT TO WHICH THIS CERTIFICATE MAY BE ISSUED OR MAY PERTAIN, THE INSURANCE AFFORDED BY THE POLICIES DESCRIBED HEREIN IS SUBJECT TO ALL THE TERMS, EXCLUSIONS AND CONDITIONS OF SUCH POLICIES. LIMITS SHOWN MAY HAVE BEEN REDUCED BY PAID CLAIMS.

INSR LTR	TYPE OF INSURANCE	ADDL INSD	SUBR WVD	POLICY NUMBER	POLICY EFF (MM/DD/YYYY)	POLICY EXP (MM/DD/YYYY)	LIMITS	
A	**COMMERCIAL GENERAL LIABILITY** ☐ CLAIMS-MADE ☐ OCCUR						EACH OCCURRENCE	$
							DAMAGE TO RENTED PREMISES (Ea occurrence)	$
							MED EXP (Any one person)	$
							PERSONAL & ADV INJURY	$
	GEN'L AGGREGATE LIMIT APPLIES PER: ☐ POLICY ☐ PROJECT ☐ LOC OTHER:						GENERAL AGGREGATE	$
							PRODUCTS - COMP/OP AGG	$
								$
B	**AUTOMOBILE LIABILITY** ☐ ANY AUTO ☐ OWNED AUTOS ONLY ☐ SCHEDULED AUTOS ☐ HIRED AUTOS ONLY ☐ NON-OWNED AUTOS ONLY						COMBINED SINGLE LIMIT (Ea accident)	$
							BODILY INJURY (Per person)	$
							BODILY INJURY (Per accident)	$
							PROPERTY DAMAGE (Per accident)	$
							PIP	$
	☐ **UMBRELLA LIAB** ☐ OCCUR ☐ **EXCESS LIAB** ☐ CLAIMS-MADE DED ☐ RETENTION $						EACH OCCURRENCE	$
							AGGREGATE	$
								$
	WORKERS COMPENSATION AND EMPLOYERS' LIABILITY Y/N ANY PROPRIETOR/PARTNER/EXECUTIVE OFFICER/MEMBER EXCLUDED? ☐ (Mandatory in NH) If yes, describe under DESCRIPTION OF OPERATIONS below		N/A				☐ PER STATUTE ☐ OTHER	
							E.L. EACH ACCIDENT	$
							E.L. DISEASE - EA EMPLOYEE	$
							E.L. DISEASE - POLICY LIMIT	$
C	Motor Truck Cargo Reefer Breakdown Included						Per Occurrence	

DESCRIPTION OF OPERATIONS / LOCATIONS / VEHICLES (Additional Remarks Schedule, may be attached if more space is required)
MC Number   Equipment information

CERTIFICATE HOLDER

Broker name
Address

CANCELLATION

SHOULD ANY OF THE ABOVE DESCRIBED POLICIES BE CANCELLED BEFORE THE EXPIRATION DATE THEREOF, NOTICE WILL BE DELIVERED IN ACCORDANCE WITH THE POLICY PROVISIONS.

AUTHORIZED REPRESENTATIVE

Example

Form **W-9**
(Rev. October 2018)
Department of the Treasury
Internal Revenue Service

Request for Taxpayer Identification Number and Certification

▶ Go to *www.irs.gov/FormW9* for instructions and the latest information.

Give Form to the requester. Do not send to the IRS.

Print or type.
See **Specific Instructions** on page 3.

1 Name (as shown on your income tax return). Name is required on this line; do not leave this line blank.

2 Business name/disregarded entity name, if different from above

3 Check appropriate box for federal tax classification of the person whose name is entered on line 1. Check only **one** of the following seven boxes.

☐ Individual/sole proprietor or single-member LLC ☐ C Corporation ☐ S Corporation ☐ Partnership ☐ Trust/estate

☐ Limited liability company. Enter the tax classification (C=C corporation, S=S corporation, P=Partnership) ▶ _____

Note: Check the appropriate box in the line above for the tax classification of the single-member owner. Do not check LLC if the LLC is classified as a single-member LLC that is disregarded from the owner unless the owner of the LLC is another LLC that is **not** disregarded from the owner for U.S. federal tax purposes. Otherwise, a single-member LLC that is disregarded from the owner should check the appropriate box for the tax classification of its owner.

☐ Other (see instructions) ▶

4 Exemptions (codes apply only to certain entities, not individuals; see instructions on page 3):

Exempt payee code (if any) _____

Exemption from FATCA reporting code (if any) _____

(Applies to accounts maintained outside the U.S.)

5 Address (number, street, and apt. or suite no.) See instructions.

6 City, state, and ZIP code

Requester's name and address (optional)

7 List account number(s) here (optional)

Part I Taxpayer Identification Number (TIN)

Enter your TIN in the appropriate box. The TIN provided must match the name given on line 1 to avoid backup withholding. For individuals, this is generally your social security number (SSN). However, for a resident alien, sole proprietor, or disregarded entity, see the instructions for Part I, later. For other entities, it is your employer identification number (EIN). If you do not have a number, see *How to get a TIN*, later.

Note: If the account is in more than one name, see the instructions for line 1. Also see *What Name and Number To Give the Requester* for guidelines on whose number to enter.

Social security number

| | | – | | | – | | | | |

or

Employer identification number

| | | – | | | | | | | |

Part II Certification

Under penalties of perjury, I certify that:

1. The number shown on this form is my correct taxpayer identification number (or I am waiting for a number to be issued to me); and
2. I am not subject to backup withholding because: (a) I am exempt from backup withholding, or (b) I have not been notified by the Internal Revenue Service (IRS) that I am subject to backup withholding as a result of a failure to report all interest or dividends, or (c) the IRS has notified me that I am no longer subject to backup withholding; and
3. I am a U.S. citizen or other U.S. person (defined below); and
4. The FATCA code(s) entered on this form (if any) indicating that I am exempt from FATCA reporting is correct.

Certification instructions. You must cross out item 2 above if you have been notified by the IRS that you are currently subject to backup withholding because you have failed to report all interest and dividends on your tax return. For real estate transactions, item 2 does not apply. For mortgage interest paid, acquisition or abandonment of secured property, cancellation of debt, contributions to an individual retirement arrangement (IRA), and generally, payments other than interest and dividends, you are not required to sign the certification, but you must provide your correct TIN. See the instructions for Part II, later.

Sign Here Signature of U.S. person ▶   Date ▶

General Instructions

Section references are to the Internal Revenue Code unless otherwise noted.

Future developments. For the latest information about developments related to Form W-9 and its instructions, such as legislation enacted after they were published, go to *www.irs.gov/FormW9*.

Purpose of Form

An individual or entity (Form W-9 requester) who is required to file an information return with the IRS must obtain your correct taxpayer identification number (TIN) which may be your social security number (SSN), individual taxpayer identification number (ITIN), adoption taxpayer identification number (ATIN), or employer identification number (EIN), to report on an information return the amount paid to you, or other amount reportable on an information return. Examples of information returns include, but are not limited to, the following.

• Form 1099-INT (interest earned or paid)

• Form 1099-DIV (dividends, including those from stocks or mutual funds)

• Form 1099-MISC (various types of income, prizes, awards, or gross proceeds)

• Form 1099-B (stock or mutual fund sales and certain other transactions by brokers)

• Form 1099-S (proceeds from real estate transactions)

• Form 1099-K (merchant card and third party network transactions)

• Form 1098 (home mortgage interest), 1098-E (student loan interest), 1098-T (tuition)

• Form 1099-C (canceled debt)

• Form 1099-A (acquisition or abandonment of secured property)

Use Form W-9 only if you are a U.S. person (including a resident alien), to provide your correct TIN.

If you do not return Form W-9 to the requester with a TIN, you might be subject to backup withholding. See *What is backup withholding,* later.

Example

RE: ▬▬▬▬▬▬▬▬▬▬▬▬▬▬▬▬▬▬▬▬▬▬

NOTICE OF ASSIGNMENT OF ACCOUNTS RECEIVABLE

Attention: Accounts Payable Supervisor

We are pleased to advise you that ▬▬▬▬▬▬▬▬▬▬▬▬▬ has entered into an agreement with ▬▬▬▬▬▬ (▬▬▬▬▬) for certain financial accommodations to obtain working capital. The availability of ▬▬▬▬▬ relationship will assist ▬▬▬▬▬▬▬▬▬▬▬▬▬ in supporting the growth and development of its business while maintaining a high level of customer service.

As part of the ▬▬▬▬ relationship, all of ▬▬▬▬▬▬▬▬▬▬▬▬▬ present and future accounts have been assigned to ▬▬▬▬ and accordingly, all payments for ▬▬▬▬▬▬▬▬▬▬▬▬▬ now or in the future, must be made directly to ▬▬▬▬▬▬▬▬▬▬ and not to ▬▬▬▬▬▬ TRUCKING or any other entity. ▬▬▬▬▬ security interest has been duly recorded by its filing under Article 9 of the Uniform Commercial Code (the "UCC"). All payments are now to be made payable to ▬▬▬▬ FACTORING, LLC pursuant to the UCC and remitted as follows:

PAYMENTS VIA MAIL

For the account of: ▬▬▬▬▬▬▬
▬▬▬▬▬ TRUCKING
PO BOX ▬▬▬

ELECTRONIC PAYMENTS
Name: ▬▬▬▬▬▬
Account No.: ▬▬▬▬▬▬
KeyBank N.A. ABA ▬▬▬▬▬▬
Benefit of: ▬▬▬▬▬▬
Remittance: ▬▬▬▬@▬▬▬.com

Payment to ▬▬▬▬▬▬▬▬▬▬ or any other entity will not discharge your obligation to pay ▬▬▬▬▬ and upon receipt of this Notice of Assignment, your failure to cause payments to be made directly to ▬▬▬▬ as set forth above may result in your liability to ▬▬▬▬ for second payment. To assist us with remittances, please indicate your company and Motor Carrier Number in the space below and return a copy of this notice to us by fax at ▬▬▬▬ or email at ▬▬▬▬▬ together with any corrections to your contact information.

This notice of assignment shall remain in effect until you are notified in writing by an officer of ▬▬▬▬▬▬▬▬ of its termination. Please notify ▬▬▬▬ at ▬▬▬▬▬ or ▬▬▬▬▬▬ if there are any adjustments to be made to an invoice or if questions arise concerning your billing. We thank you in advance for your cooperation, and we look forward to the continued growth and prosperity of ▬▬▬▬▬▬▬▬▬▬▬.

▬▬▬▬▬▬▬▬▬▬ (Jan 7, 2016)

▬▬▬▬▬▬▬▬▬▬▬▬▬, President

Please complete and return via email to noa@fleetone.com or via fax to ▬▬▬▬	
Received by:	Company Name:
Position:	Motor Carrier Number:
Phone:	Address:
Fax:	City/St./Zip

14

Express Accounts Purchase Agreement ▬▬▬▬ Page 8 Client Initials ▬▬

DISPATCHER DUTIES OVERVIEW

A dispatcher must have good written and verbal communication skills. Your main role as a dispatcher will be viewing information about loads posted on the load board and negotiating rates for your truck. When you call for details about a load, the information will be communicated quickly and you must listen, think, and write simultaneously. You are listening for information about the load such as date, pickup time, product, weight, number of picks and drops, delivery date and time, and any special requirements about the load. Sometimes the information posted on the load board is inaccurate in regards to pickup locations or weight of product.

You will also spend a significant part of your time submitting requests for certificates of insurance and completing carrier packets, which usually should take about 15 minutes to complete. The carrier packet is an application a broker sends to the motor carrier via email. You must provide the motor carrier name, address, phone number, email address, MC#, DOT#, Notice of Assignment (if applicable), banking information–to include a voided check, and information about the equipment and lanes the truck travels. In addition to the packet, you will need to send a copy of the motor carrier's operating authority, certificate of insurance, W-9, and notice of assignment--if the carrier is set up with a factoring company. Some carrier packets are electronic and the setup process takes less time.

After you have completed the setup packet for your motor carrier and emailed it back to the broker, you will receive a rate confirmation about 15-20 minutes later. It is very important to read the rate confirmation and verify all the information is correct. Look to see if there are any pickup numbers for the load. Always ask about a pickup number because sometimes it will not be on the rate confirmation sheet. If there is a discrepancy, contact the broker immediately and allow them to send a corrected rate confirmation. If all the information is correct, sign the rate confirmation and email it back to the broker. While dispatching, you should call your motor carrier and relay the pickup number and any important information about the load. A copy of the rate confirmation should be sent to the motor carrier's email address.

Now the motor carrier has everything needed to transport the load. The motor carrier is responsible for making sure the PO#'s on the BOL from the shipper match the PO#s on the rate confirmation. If there are any discrepancies, the carrier should notify you immediately. Your motor carrier should give you updates about ETA's to the shipper and receiver as well as in and out times. Some brokers will send a tracking link like macropoint or trucker tools to the motor carrier's cell phone and all the motor carrier has to do is click on the link and the broker can track the load remotely.

Once the motor carrier has delivered the load, both the receiver (consignee) and motor carrier should sign the bill of lading (BOL). The motor carrier should then send scanned copies (pdf files) of ALL pages of the paperwork to the dispatcher, unless the broker requests original paperwork.

Operating Authorities

You can do a simple check of the motor carrier's authority by visiting https://safer.fmcsa.dot.gov, and entering the MC# or DOT# to verify if the number is still active. Some brokers will not work with new authorities that have not been active for at least 90 days. Depending on the broker, this number may be 90 days active, or 180 days active. Companies like Total Quality Logistics and CH Robinson work with new authorities. Check with each broker to know their requirements before you book a load.

EQUIPMENT TYPES

As a dispatcher, you might work with 1 or 2 equipment types on a regular basis. For example, when I started as a dispatcher for my husband's trucking company, I had to become familiar with the refrigerated trailer, or "reefer" in short. I feel most comfortable negotiating freight rates with this equipment type because I learned about its features and the products it can transport.

The more you learn about equipment and the products it can carry, the better you will become at negotiating rates for your truck. Things I listen for when talking with a broker about a refrigerated load include temperature. For example, a refrigerated load should pay more than a dry van load because it will require fuel to run the refrigeration unit and there is more liability. Also, the product is very important. Products like ice cream, seafood, apples, bananas, and berries are considered "high dollar" loads. Some motor carriers will not transport certain products because of the liability they might incur from the product being damaged or rejected.

There have been times when I dispatched for a flatbed, or power only, but I stick with refrigerated and dry van equipment because I feel most comfortable dispatching this type of equipment. I would suggest picking 1 to 2 equipment types and becoming an "expert" about its features and the freight it can transport. I have provided a list of equipment for you to review. These are not all the equipment types, but I feel these are probably the ones you will most likely dispatch.

Flatbed Trailer

Refrigerated Trailer

Step-deck Trailer

Dry Van Trailer

Tractor with Sleeper

Vented Dry Van Trailer

Day Cab

Tarps with Straps

Swing Doors

Air-Chute

Etracks

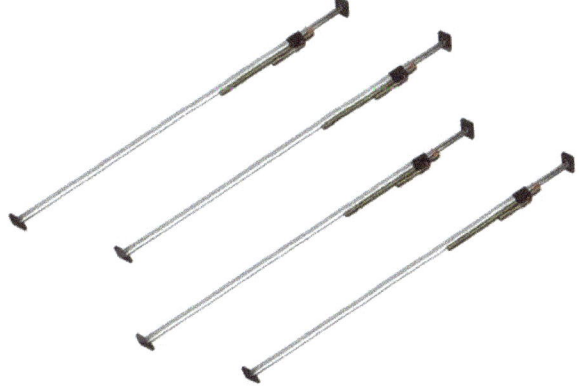
Load Locks

HOW MUCH SHOULD YOUR TRUCK MAKE?

When you are working with a motor carrier, you can help them think about how to set their truck rates. The answer to how much a truck should make depends on the business operating and living expenses. Some motor carriers don't have equipment payments, while others do. Some may not have a mortgage payment, while others do. The simplest way I can explain is to add up all your business expenses which can include insurance, equipment notes, load board subscriptions, accounting, and revolving business credit card accounts for things like fuel and maintenance. Then add all your monthly living expenses which can include rent/mortgage, utilities, food, car note, and insurance. Add those two numbers together and that is what your truck should aim to make per week.

My reasoning for the "per week" amount is that if you run into mechanical or health issues and you or the truck are down for a week or two, you would at least have your expenses covered for the month. Also it is a way for you to start creating an emergency fund for your business if you don't have one already. For me, I use the same guidelines of Dave Ramsey's baby steps for my husband's trucking business. Motor carriers should have at least 3-6 months of business emergency funds in their business checking account. If your number is really high, this means that you should really utilize the tools on the load board to learn about the areas of the country where there is a demand for your type of equipment.

When I started to look at our expenses-the numbers, it really allowed me to be more intentional when searching for loads. I could hear myself think aloud, "if I take this load, it is going to get me to my halfway point of what we need to make", or "this load is too cheap and will take up too much time".

Here are some questions you can ask your motor carrier in regards to setting rates for the truck?

1. What type of equipment do you have?
2. What is the maximum weight you will carry?
3. How many miles per gallon does your truck get?

4. How long have you had your authority?
5. What is your $ per mile rate?
6. How much money do you need to make in a week? Month?
7. What states DO YOU NOT travel?
8. Are you tanker endorsed?
9. Do you have a twic card?
10. Are you hazmat endorsed?
11. Can you run -10 or -20? (for refrigerated trailers)
12. Do you have air chutes? (for refrigerated trailers)
13. Does your trailer have e-tracks?
14. Do you carry load locks? How many?
15. Do you keep straps? How many?
16. Do you have tarps and chains? What sizes and how many? (for flatbed)
17. Are there any items you will not transport?

LOAD BOARD NAVIGATION

To start dispatching, you will need internet access to a load board. There are many load boards on the market. My top two contenders are TruckersEdge and Truckstop.com. If you have a legal Dispatching business with a EIN# and business structure setup, you can contact these companies directly and inquire about their dispatching packages. If you are a motor carrier with an MC#, Trucker Tools has a load board you can access free of charge. Both TruckersEdge and Truckstop.com offer load board subscriptions I think are reasonably priced.

Many brokerages offer free in house load boards that you can have access to once you set up as a motor carrier with their company. Other brokerages will send you an email of their load list. Examples of brokerages who offer their own load boards are:

1. CH Robinson
2. Total Quality Logistics
3. Coyote Logistics
4. Convoy app
5. Uber Freight app

I would also like to add that there are many loads that never get posted to the load board. Independent motor carriers with active operating authorities should find, build and maintain relationships with their customers. Also building a healthy relationship with a broker can help you stay consistent. If you are in a specific lane that you have run before, followup with the broker and let them know your truck's availability.

The load board is where you can get information about freight moving across the United States. You will want to spend some time becoming familiar with its tools and how to use them to negotiate a more competitive rate. The load board will allow you to input data about origin city and state, date availability, and destination city and state. Make sure you select the type of equipment you are dispatching. Depending on the load board you use, you can get 7 day, 15 day, or 30 day lane rate averages.

Scenario: Frank is empty in Atlanta, GA. He has a 53 foot dry van. Frank's minimum dollar per mile rate is $2.50. It is always important to keep in mind we are trying to get as much for the truck as we can. His truck gets 5.7 miles per gallon of fuel. The price of diesel fuel is $3.799 per gallon.

Load boards will have a main page where you can input information about the origin and/or destination. You do not have to enter a destination. As an example, I will be using Atlanta, Georgia as the origin. The equipment type I will enter is a dry van. The equipment type defaults to reefer. I am going to change that option to a dry van.

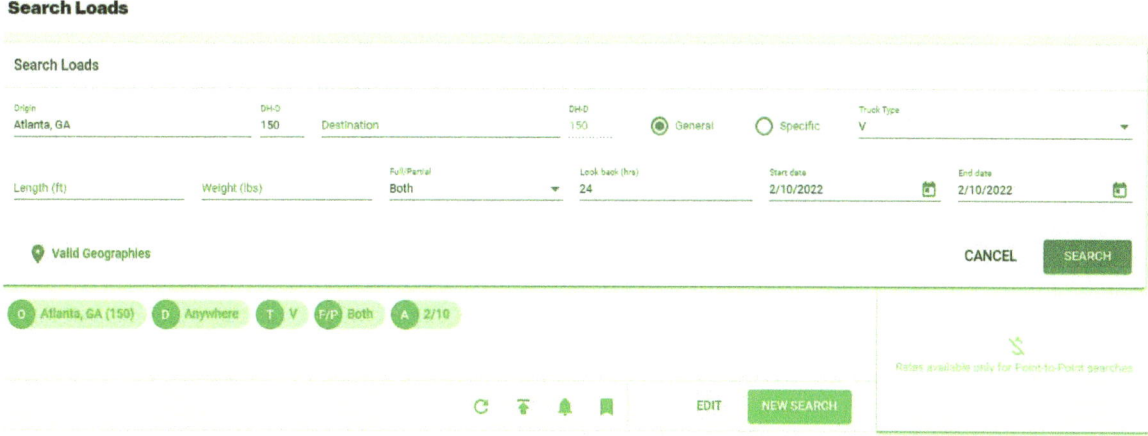

Now you can see, the origin is Atlanta, Georgia. I have entered 150 as the number of miles the truck is willing to travel for his or her next pickup. Usually you can find a reload within a 70 mile radius. My rule of thumb is not to have the motor carrier drive more than 100 miles to the next pick, but there may be times when the truck has to travel more than 100 miles. The date has been set to 2/10/22. Now we can search to see how many loads originate from Atlanta, Georgia on this particular date.

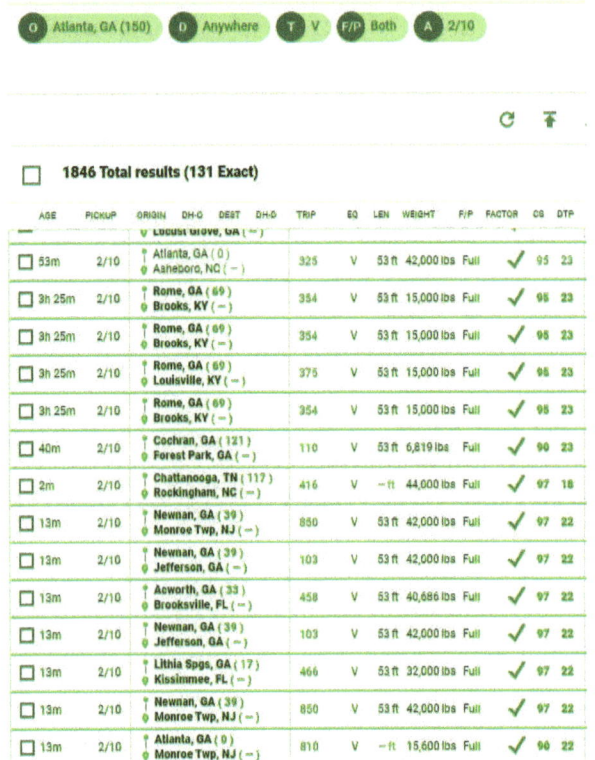

There are over 1800 dry van loads picking up out of Atlanta! We are taking a snapshot and only viewing the loads on the left. Before you call on a load you must do a little homework. Calculate a rate.

In this example, let's select Atlanta, GA to Asheboro, NC. It is 325 loaded miles.

Let's see what happens when we select this option.

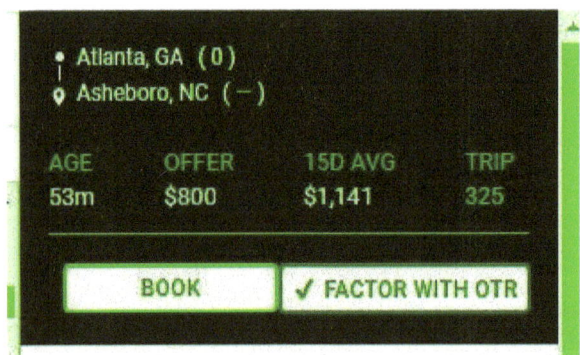

For this particular lane, the broker has this load posted for $800. The 15 day average for this lane is $1141, so there is room for negotiating. Here are some things to consider when negotiating a rate:

1. equipment type
2. product
3. weight
4. temperature, (for refrigerated trailers)
5. capacity
6. pick up time and location
7. delivery time and location
8. distance

9. number of days product is on the truck
10. weekend pick
11. holiday pick
12. expedited pick
13. weather conditions
14. # picks and or drops
15. Diesel fuel prices

SETTING RATES

Before I call on any load, I like to do a little homework and make use of the tools my load board offers me.

The first tool I like to view are the National averages for the equipment I am dispatching. DAT offers DAT Trendlines for reefer, flat bed, and dry van equipment free of charge. These are only averages and your truck might be in a lane that is above or below the National Average. Atlanta, GA is in the southeast region and the National Average for this region is about $2.91 for dry van equipment. You can use these numbers as guidelines.

I also want to note that DAT regularly posts videos about market conditions and how it is affecting the industry. I would highly suggest viewing those videos to stay informed about what is happening in the industry.

My load board has a tool called "load to truck ratios". The load to truck ratios allow me to see what states need the equipment type I am dispatching. I use this tool every day to give me a general idea of the capacity. Capacity fluctuates throughout the day. If you review this chart throughout the day, you will see how quickly things change.

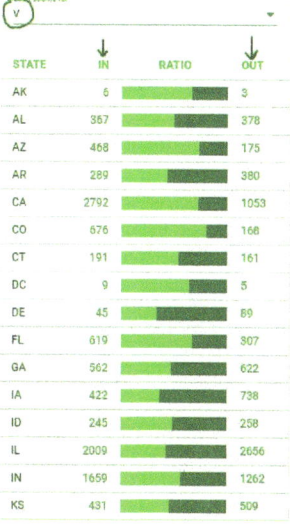

For our example, we are using Atlanta, GA. According to this chart, there are 562 trucks bringing loads into the state of Georgia and 622 trucks transporting loads out of Georgia. This tells me that there are about the same amount of loads entering and leaving the state. But now we have to take a closer look at the lane we are interested in: Atlanta, GA to Asheboro, NC.

The next feature I take advantage of is the quick rate look up. I can enter the origin and destination and get a general idea of the lane average.

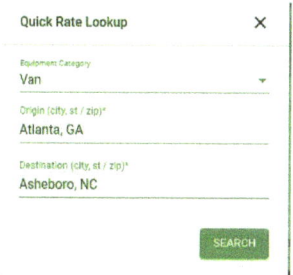

Atlanta, GA is our origin and Asheboro, NC is our destination. Our equipment type if dry van.

Things to consider when you are setting a rate?

- What is this going to cost me in fuel?
- Is this a toll route? How much is it going to cost?
- Am I going into a lane where my equipment is in demand?
- How far will I have to travel for my next reload?
- Am I going to shipper/receiver who takes too long to load/unload?
- Broker fees (quickpay, fuel advance)

	BROKER-TO-CARRIER SPOT	SHIPPER-TO-CARRIER CONTRACT
Atlanta Mkt - Greensboro Mkt (325 mi)		
15 Day Avg:	$1,141 ($3.51/mi)	
Range:	$991 - $1,219 ($3.05 - $3.75/mi)	

The quick rate lookup feature shows the average for this lane. This gives me a range of $991 to $1219. The broker has this load posted for $800. This rate tells me that the broker has a lot of time to find a truck, or there are more trucks than loads in this lane. Let's do some quick math to calculate the dollar per mile.

Rate ÷ number of miles = $ per mile rate

$800 ÷ 325 = $2.46 per mile

In our case, we are going to $1219 as our baseline.

In our example, we need to know how much fuel it will cost Frank's truck to transport the load. Frank's truck gets 5.7 miles per gallon. Diesel fuel costs $3.799 a gallon.

(Number of loaded miles ÷ miles per gallon)

(325 ÷ 5.7) = 57.0175438596 gallons of fuel

(gallon of fuel x fuel price)= fuel expense

57.0715438596 x 3.799 = $216.61 (rounded to the nearest hundredth)

It will cost $216.61 in fuel to transport from Atlanta, GA to Asheboro NC.

Now let's add the minimum rate and the cost of fuel:

$1219 + $216.61 = $1435.61

Next, we can round up this number to $1500 and increase this amount by at least 10% to 30% depending on what is happening in the market. $1500 is what I would like to get for this load, but when negotiating I will start with a higher number.

$$\$1500 \times .10 = \$150$$
$$\$1500 + \$150 = \$1650$$

If I am interested in this load, I would select the lane and somewhere on the screen is more information about the load. The box will also provide company information. If I am not set up with the broker, I would contact the factoring company by email, or login to a database provided by the factoring company to conduct a credit check on the broker's MC#. If the credit check is approved, you can contact the broker to learn more about the load. If you are not set up with a factoring company you will need to do some additional work before booking the load.

PICK UP DATE	2/10
PICK UP HOURS	—
DOCK HOURS	—
FULL/PARTIAL	Full
TRUCK	Van
LENGTH	53 ft
WEIGHT	8,689 lbs
COMMODITY	—
COMMENTS	PU 02/10 10:00 DEL 02/11 12:30
REFERENCE #	8-179920

We don't know any of the specific details about this load, only that it is 8,689 pounds. A dry van truck can transport 44-45,000 pounds. In our scenario, the broker says he runs this load every day for $1300. If it is a simple 1 pick 1 drop load picking up and delivering to a shipper and receiver who loads and unloads fairly quickly, you can counter the offer by stating you have a truck empty now in Atlanta and can book the load right now for $1650. The broker counters the offer and says $1400. What do you do? If this is a lane you are very familiar with and you know you can get $1650, stay firm on your offer. Bottom line is it is your decision. In our scenario, we booked the load for $1550.00.

$$\text{Rate} \div \text{number of miles} = \$ \text{ per mile rate}$$
$$\$1550 \div 325 = \$4.76$$
$4.76 is higher than the National Average.

But what if the broker is firm and says that $1300 is the best rate he or she can offer? You have two options, you can either accept the offer or you can look for something else. Don't feel pressured to accept an offer you don't want, especially if you are familiar with a lane that you run often. Stay firm with your initial offer and say I'm sorry but $1650 is the best I can do. If necessary, you can explain about what it's going to cost in fuel and other things you know about the load to support your rate. They will either accept or reject the offer. There are times when I stay firm with my offer and end the conversation, only to have the broker call back and ask if the truck is still available. Remember your goal is to make as much for the truck as possible!

The more you practice using the tools and understand how they help you with your rates, the better you will become at negotiating. Pay attention to industry news and how it affects the market. Let your quality service of on time pickup up and delivery and consistent communication be your bargaining power. If the Operating Authority is new, don't be afraid to ask for the rate you need. Consider all the expenses like fuel, insurance, maintenance, and time.

BOOKING A LOAD

When you make the call to a broker, you will state your name, company, and the lane and reference # from the load board. They will ask for your MC#, and then start to tell the details about the load. You should already have a set rate in your head. Make sure to record date, pickup times, product, weight, and any special requirements in a notebook. Never tell them your rate! Let the broker make an offer first if the rate is not posted. If they ask what you can do this for, clarify the details of the load and ask about lane averages. Ask questions about things you don't understand.

Before you make a commitment, here are some important questions you need to ask if you are not set up with a factoring company.

A. Questions to Ask

    1. I want to book this load but I am not set up as a carrier-usually they will ask how long have you had your authority. Know how long the Authority has been active.

    2. How do you pay? (They may say net 30 days)

    3. Do you offer quickpay? 1 day? 2 day? If so, what are the terms and fees?

    4. How do I get setup for quickpay?- (they should send a quickpay form)

    5. Do you offer fuel advances? What is the percentage and fee?(usually the advance is a percentage of the rate plus a fee, i.e 50% of the rate and a 3% fee of the rate)

    6. Do you pay your trucks detention?

Where would you like me to send that packet? (or the carrier link)

You can send it to (your dispatching email @gmail.com)

B. Rate confirmation

If there are any verbal changes to the rate confirmation, you should always get an updated rate confirmation from the broker. If it is not on the rate confirmation, it doesn't exist. If you are set up with a factoring company, contact them and provide the broker's MC # to get approval first. Do not book a load without conducting a credit check, or asking questions about the details of the load and payment methods first. If a broker cancels on a load after your truck has been dispatched, they should email you a new rate confirmation for a "truck ordered not used". The amount varies from $150-$250.

C. Quickpay

Many motor carriers can not wait net 30 days to get paid for a load. Brokers provide motor carriers with payment options called "QUICKPAY" and take a small percentage from the rate so that the motor carrier can receive payment within 1-7 business days. Quickpay terms and fees vary from broker to broker and can range from 1.5% to 5%. If a Broker can not offer quickpay, the motor carrier has some options.

Option 1: Wait the net 30 days for the broker to pay.

Option 2: Look for another broker who offers quickpay.

Option 3: Factor the load with a factoring company.

D. Factoring Company

Some motor carriers may already be set up with a factoring company. The factoring company buys an invoice for a small fee and pays the motor carrier within 1-2 business days. Before you book a load, you can contact the factoring company to run a "credit check" on the broker by providing the broker's MC#. Most factoring companies have an online system where a motor carrier can create an account to run a credit check. If the broker has a good history of paying invoices, the factoring company will extend a line of credit to the broker. Once the load is completed, a factoring schedule, along with a copy of the motor carrier's invoice, rate confirmation, signed BOLS, and lumpers (if applicable) are submitted to the factoring company instead of the broker. The factoring company waits net 30, or 45 days to receive payment from the broker. I have provided a list of SOME factoring companies, but do your research first.

Factoring Companies:

1. TBS Factoring
2. Wex Fleet One
3. Love's
4. OTR Factoring
5. APEX Factoring

E. Fuel Advances

Many new motor carriers starting out request a fuel advance to transport a load. Before you agree to transport a load, you need to ask if the broker offers fuel advance. Some brokers will advance the motor carrier a percentage of the rate once the truck is loaded. The fuel advance can be 40-50% of the rate. If an advance is needed, email the broker (with the load # in the subject line) along with a clear copy, (in pdf format), of the BOL which proves the product is on the truck, and indicate the amount needed for the fuel advance. The broker will send a code. The code can be given to most truck stops to purchase fuel and in some cases receive cash back.

If you are requesting a fuel advance, email the broker a clear copy of the BOL from the shipper with a request for fuel advance.

Subject: Load 123435 Fuel Advance

Body: Requesting a fuel advance for $(whatever amount you need)
Please see attached BOL.

Thank you
Motor Carrier Name
MC#

F. Lumper

Some loads require a lumper. A lumper is a service to unload a truck. The amount of the lumper is usually not known until the truck is unloaded. Some lumper services send a link to the motor carrier's phone with the amount for the lumper. Notify the broker of the amount and a code is issued. The motor carrier enters the code into the link. Once the fee is paid, a receipt is issued and must be submitted with the proof of delivery. Some receivers have prepaid accounts set up to avoid the time and hassle. If the motor carrier decides to pay upfront, this amount will be added to the rate minus the quickpay or factoring fee. Always ask for a receipt to submit with paperwork.

If you are requesting a lumper, email the broker with a request for a lumper.

Subject: Load 123435 Lumper Request

Body: The lumper fee is $(lumper fee amount)

Thank you
Motor Carrier Name
MC#

Comchecks, and t-checks have become out-dated. Express codes are more common. I thought I would include an example of these checks just in case someone asks about it. If it is a comcheck, enter the motor carrier's company name, date, amount, and Broker's name. Leave the box marked "authorization number" blank. Enter express code that the broker provided, the driver's phone number, state, and Driver's license number. The motor carrier takes the comcheck to the truck stop and the attendant calls the 800 number listed on the check to obtain the authorization number and writes that number in the box labeled "authorization number".

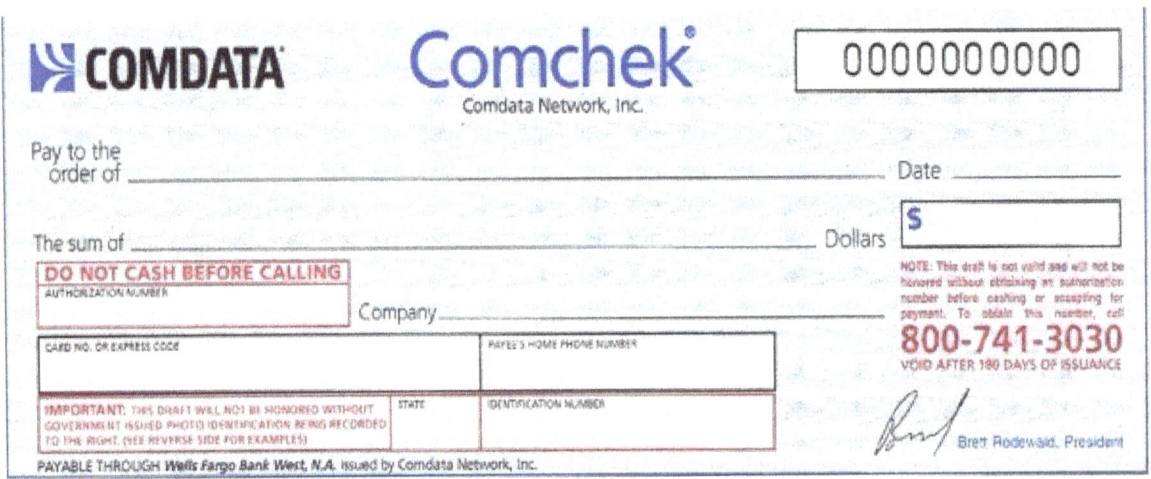

Note: the motor carrier completes the comcheck, not the dispatcher. The dispatcher requests the express code.

Note: the motor carrier completes the comcheck, not the dispatcher. The dispatcher requests the express code.

G. Check Calls

Brokers make check calls to keep track of the location of the load. To limit the number of check calls, email the broker with updates about:

      1. ETA to shipper
      2. Check in time at shipper
      3. Loaded at shipper (check out time) and ETA to receiver
      4. Check in time at receiver
      5. Unloaded and check out time at receiver

H. Time and Detention

It is very important the truck you are dispatching arrives at his or her scheduled appointments on time. Some brokers will charge the motor carrier for being late to an appointment. It is extremely important the motor carrier gets into the habit of recording the time in and time out at both the shipper and receiver. The unspoken rule is to give a shipper or receiver 2 hours to load or unload a truck unless the rate confirmation indicates otherwise, but this may not always be the case. After the 2 hour mark, notify the broker about detention start time, and the motor carrier can start charging for detention.

The reality is your motor carrier will spend time waiting at the shipper or receiver to get loaded or unloaded. Some brokers indicate on the rate confirmations they do not pay for detention. Sometimes the motor carrier may not get detention at all and if they do, it is not worth the time spent waiting. If you are waiting to get loaded and 2 hours have passed, immediately make the broker aware. Usually they will tell you that they will call their customer. If another hour passes, make the broker aware you arrived on time for the scheduled appointment. I also want to note that certain products require longer than usual wait times. For example, fresh produce is notorious for taking hours to get loaded because sometimes the product is still being harvested. Produce products like watermelons do not pay detention. Flowers (nursery) are another type of product that does not pay for detention.

This is why it is important to know your product, and consider these factors while you are negotiating your rate. My rule of thumb is to at least make an attempt to get detention for your trucks even if you don't receive it. If you are at the receiver waiting to get unloaded, try your best to communicate with the broker your check in time. Ideally, after you have unloaded, the broker should send you an updated rate confirmation with the detention added, but this does not always happen. The broker might explain they need to get detention approval from their customer and it could take a week or so if it is approved. If your motor carrier wants to get paid immediately, they might not want to wait on the approval. Again, I would make an attempt to get detention.

Example: Detention Request by email

Subject: Load 123435 Detention

Body: Requesting detention
    Check in (enter time)
    Appointment time (enter time)
    Check out: (enter time)

Please send an updated rate confirmation for detention at the shipper (or receiver)

    Thank you
    Motor Carrier Name
    MC#

REQUESTING A CERTIFICATE OF INSURANCE

Your motor carrier should provide you with a copy of his or her certificate of insurance. You need to verify that the insurance has not expired. Check the expiration date on the certificate! Your motor carrier should notify you immediately of any policy changes to the insurance. When you need to list a broker as a certificate holder, you can either call or email the insurance company listed on the certificate. Some insurance companies have a portal motor carriers can access to submit their own certificates. Once your request has been made it should take about 15 minutes to receive a copy. I always request the certificate first, and then begin the carrier packet. By the time I have completed the packet, I should have a copy of the certificate. The insurance company usually emails a copy to you and the broker. Some brokers want the certificate directly from the insurance company.

If you will be dispatching a truck, you and the motor carrier should contact the insurance company and explain that you can request certificates on behalf of your motor carrier.

W-9 Quick Tip

I use Adobe fill and sign to complete the motor carrier's W-9. To cut down time I have forms like the W-9 already prefilled with the motor carrier's information. The only thing I have to change is the date. In my experience, I always use an EIN# and never a motor carrier's social security number. This form is quite simple to complete. The part that is sometimes overlooked when completing is entity classification. Be sure to choose one: LLC, C-Corp, S-corp, partnership, or trust.

Example: Certificate Request by Phone

Hi, this is (your name) with (motor carrier's company name).

I need to request a certificate of insurance.

What's the name of insured?

Name of Motor Carrier's Company.

Who's the certificate holder?

Certificate holder is (the broker- you need to provide the Broker's name (ie. TQL) and company address. This information will go at the bottom of the certificate.)

Can you send a copy to (certificate holders) email address and my email address. Thank you

  A copy should be sent to the broker and your email address

EXAMPLE: CERTIFICATE REQUEST BY EMAIL

Subject: Certificate Request

Body: Name of insured Frank Doe-Speedy Express Trucking

    Certificate Holder

    Total Quality Logistics

    Address Info

Please email a copy to jdoe@tql.com

Thank you

COMPLETING A CARRIER SETUP PACKET

The broker's setup packet will be sent via email in a pdf format or electronic link. The broker's packet should include information about the broker which can include the broker's authority, surety bond, credit references, and W-9, along with a carrier application. You will have to complete the application with the motors carrier's information. The packet should have a cover page that explains all the documents needed to set up the carrier and where to send the completed packet. I have provided you with a sample packet for your review. Some packets will require information about what states and lanes the truck travels.

Carrier Packet Steps

1. Request the certificate (takes about 15 minutes after request is made)
2. Fill out carrier packet
3. Complete W-9
4. Gather supporting documents (you should have a certificate by now)

    - Operating Authority (pdf)
    - Certificate of Insurance (pdf)
    - W-9 (pdf)
    - Carrier setup packet (pdf)

5. Merge all documents and email to broker

EXAMPLE LOGISTICS

Dear Valued Carrier,

Thank you for your interest in Example Logistics.

In order to qualify you will need the following documents:

- ✓ Signed Broker-Carrier Agreement - make sure to sign and fill out completely

- ✓ Completed W-9 - a blank W-9 has been included for your convenience (if needed)

- ✓ Worker's Compensation Insurance Copy

- ✓ Copy of MC Authority Document

- ✓ New Carrier Profile (attached)

- ✓ Safety Rating Documentation(if available)

- ✓ Certificate of Insurance faxed back to 000-000-0000 with:
  Certificate holder listed as: Example Logistics Sample Road Anywhere, USA 00000 **** One (1) Million Auto Liability and $100,000 Cargo Insurance is REQUIRED – no exceptions****

For your convenience, we offer several options for sending the necessary documentation: email, fax, or mail. We look forward to working with you!

Example Logistics
Phone: 000-000-0000
Fax: 000-000-0000
Email: example@logistics.com
Address: 00000 Sample Road Anywhere, USA 00000

Invoices via Email: example@logistics.com

New Carrier Setup Packet

Included:
Intro/Setup Page   page 1
Broker Company Information   page 2
Carrier Profile   page 3
Broker FMCSA Form & Bond Information page 4-6
Broker W-9 Tax certification   page 7
Workman's Compensation Election   page 8
TIA Membership Certificate   page 9
Transportation Broker Carrier Agreement page 10-20
Carrier Quick Pay Options   page 21-23

EXAMPLE LOGISTICS

Contact info:

Company: Example Logistics
Address: 00000 Sample Road
Anywhere, USA 00000
000-000-0000

Invoices via Email: billing@Examplelogistics.com

Contact: Jane Doe
Web: www.examplelogistics.com

Officers/Senior Management:
John Doe - President & COO –   jdoe@examplelogistics.com

Revenue Services:
Mark Doe -   mdoe@examplelogistics.com 000-000-0000 ext 0000

Invoices via Email: billing@examplelogistics.com

Authorities:
Business Type: 3PL
MC: 000000-B
FedTaxID: 00-0000000
DUNS: 00-000-0000
Incorporated: 1800

Banking Info:
Bank: Example Bank
Contact: James Doe
000-000-0000

Carrier References:
Carrier   Contact   Location   Phone Sample Freight   John Doe   Anywhere, USA   000-000-0000 Sample Express   Jane Doe Anywhere, USA   000-000-0000 Sample Trucking   John Doe Anywhere, USA   000-000-0000

Example Logistics®
00000 Sample Road | Anywhere, USA 00000
examplelogistics.com | 0-000-000-0000

EXAMPLE LOGISTICS

SCAC CODE _____ MC#_____ US DOT#_____ FEDERAL ID#_____

Carrier Name: _____ DBA: _____

Physical Address: _____

City: _____ State: _____ Zip: _____

Website: _____

Owner/President/Principal: _____

Dispatch Contact: _____

Phone: _____ Email: _____ Fax: _____

Accounting Contact: _____

Phone: _____ Email: _____ Fax: _____

After hours number: _____

MC Number: _____ Carrier SCAC code: _____ Are you Smart Way certified? YES NO

Insurance Agent Name: _____ Phone: _____

Number of Units _____ Number of Trailers _____ Do you have EDI capability? YES or NO Do you have HAZ MAT Certification? YES or NO? How many teams do you run? _____ # of Tractors _____ # of Trailers _____ List

# of Trailers by Type: V53_____ V48_____ FB_____ R53_____

Geographic Service Area _____

**This information will be used to help us determine future opportunities that may exists based on the services your company provides.

****If your account receivables department is different than your physical address, or if you are using a factoring company, please complete below****

Receivable/ Factoring Company Name: _____

Receivable Address: _____

City: _____ State: _____ Zip: _____

Example Logistics®
00000 Sample Road | Anywhere, USA 00000
examplelogistics.com | 0-000-000-0000

EXAMPLE LOGISTICS

Workman's Compensaion Certificate of Election

CERTIFICATION

This is to certify that the firm named below has elected to not cover its owners, partners or officers under the workers' compensation laws of the State of _____. The firm named below certifies that it has no employees. The firm named below certifies that it uses no independent contractors. Based upon the election not to cover owners, partners or officers, the fact there are not other employees and that no independent contractors are used, a workers' compensation policy is not purchased.

AGREEMENT

The firm named below promises, in consideration for work received from Client, that if the owners, partners or officers choose to change their election, if any employee is hired or if any independent contractor is used, then a certificate of insurance evidencing workers' compensation coverage will be furnished prior to the commencement of any work.

PERIOD

The period of this agreement is: _____ to _____.

CARRIER

Carrier Name: _____

MC Number: _____

By: _____

Signature: _____

Title: _____

Date: _____

Example Logistics®
00000 Sample Road | Anywhere, USA 00000
examplelogistics.com | 0-000-000-0000

Example Logistics LLC
000 Example Road | Anywhere, US 00000
examplelogistics.com | 0-000-000-0000

BROKER – CARRIER AGREEMENT

This Broker – Carrier Agreement (the "Agreement") is made this _____ day of _____, 20__, by and between Example Logistics LLC, 00000 Sample Rd., Anywhere, US 00000 ("Broker"), and _____, whose business address is _____ ("Carrier") and is effective as of _____, 20___ ("Effective Date").

WHEREAS, Broker is duly licensed as a property broker to arrange for the transportation of property by motor carrier under permit MC-000000 issued by the Federal Motor Carrier Safety Administration ("FMCSA").

WHEREAS, Carrier is a duly licensed motor carrier which has been issued an operating authority by the FMCSA (or its predecessor, the ICC) that authorizes Carrier to provide transportation service for the shipments tendered to it by Broker.

NOW, THEREFORE, intending to be legally bound, the parties enter into this Agreement in accordance with 49 U.S.C. §14101(b)(1) and expressly waive any and all rights and remedies that each may have under 49 U.S.C. § 13101 through §14914 that are contrary to the specific provisions of this Agreement and agree as follows:

1. Description of Services – During the term of this Agreement, Broker agrees to tender to Carrier on a non-exclusive basis, and Carrier agrees to accept from Broker, from time-to-time, shipments consisting of certain goods for transport between points within North America. Carrier will, using due care, pick-up, as and when requested, transport in a timely manner, and deliver in good order and condition, the shipments which are tendered by Broker to Carrier, in accordance with the terms set forth in this Agreement ("Services").

Every shipment tendered to Carrier by Broker on or after the date of this Agreement will be deemed to be a tender to Carrier as a motor contract carrier and will be subject to the terms of this Agreement; Broker's Terms and Conditions, to the extent applicable which are posted online at www.examplelogistics; and applicable law. In the event of a conflict between the terms and provisions of this Agreement and the Broker's Terms and Conditions, the terms and provisions of this Agreement shall control. In the event this Agreement is silent on a particular subject, the provisions of Broker's Terms and Conditions, if applicable, shall control.

2. Carrier's Operating Authority. Carrier represents and warrants that it is fully authorized to lawfully provide the Services covered by this Agreement in all the jurisdictions covered by this Agreement, as a contract carrier of general commodities freight for interstate and intrastate transport in the United States. Carrier further represents and warrants that Exhibit A, attached hereto is a true, correct and complete copy of the required local, state, and federal operating licenses, permits and certificates of Carrier as of the date of this Agreement necessary to provide the Services. Carrier will obtain and keep in good standing during the term of this Agreement all local, state, and federal permits, licenses and registration requirements and pay any governmental charges necessary to allow the Carrier to provide the Services set forth this Agreement.

comply with or conform to provisions or orders of regulatory agencies having jurisdiction over this Agreement or the Services, results in different or additional charges for the Services, Carrier will be responsible for indemnifying Broker from such charges by paying Broker liquidated damages equal to any additional charges required to be paid, and any costs or attorneys' fees incurred by Broker in connection therewith.

4. Carrier's Operating Responsibilities – Carrier will be responsible for the procuring and operation of the vehicles it uses and the employment, training, supervision and control of the drivers and any helpers. Carrier will be responsible for safe and lawful operation of the vehicles used in the performance of the Services and will assume all costs, expenses, and liabilities incident to or arising out of furnishing, maintaining, repairing, or operating motor vehicles and other equipment, labor, fuel, supplies, and insurance. Carrier will notify Broker promptly by telephone of any accident, theft or other occurrence that impairs the safety of or delays the delivery of Broker's customer's goods.

Carrier will at all times during the term of this Agreement, maintain the highest safety rating established by any country, and if applicable, state, province or territory through which Broker's cargo will be transported, which, for purposes of this Agreement, shall mean the (a) safety rating system established by the Federal Motor Carrier Safety Administration ("FMCSA"), for motor carriers operating in the United States and/or (b) for motor carriers operating in Canada, the safety rating system established under the National Safety Code ("NSC") Safety Fitness Certificate issued by the Canadian province or territory where Carrier's vehicles are base-plated. Carrier further warrants that it holds and shall maintain during the term of this Agreement, at minimum, a "satisfactory" or "unrelated" safety rating, or a substantively equivalent rating under the Carrier Safety Management System, implemented under the FMCSA Compliance, Safety, Accountability ("CSA") program, with respect to Carrier's operations in the United States and a substantively equivalent rating under the Carrier's NSC Safety Fitness Certificate, for its operations within Canada. Carrier agrees to notify Broker immediately if the safety ratings changes, or if it is found by any governing authority to have violated any law or regulation related to safety or insurance coverage.

To the extent that any shipments subject to this Agreement are transported within the State of California on refrigerated equipment, Carrier, on behalf of shipper, consignee and broker interests, warrants that it shall only utilize equipment which is in full compliance with the California Air Resources Board (ARB) TRU ACTM in-use regulations. Carrier shall be liable to Broker for any penalties, or any other liability, imposed on, or assumed by Broker due to penalties imposed on Broker's customer because of Carrier's use of non-compliant equipment.

Carrier will perform the Services as an independent contractor and neither its employees nor agents will be deemed to be employees or agents of Broker. No authority has been conferred upon Carrier, by Broker, to hire any persons on behalf of Broker and Carrier will assume full responsibility for selecting, engaging and discharging its employees, agents, servants or helpers and for otherwise directing and controlling their services. Carrier will assume full responsibility for complying with all applicable laws and regulations for the benefit of its employees and under no circumstances will Broker be liable for the debts or obligations of Carrier for the wages, salaries, or benefits of Carrier's employees.

5. Receipts – Each shipment will be evidenced by a written form initiated by the consignor at the point of origin of the shipment in a form acceptable to Broker, and will be legibly signed by the Carrier showing the kind and quantity of the commodity received at the loading point(s) specified. Such form will be evidence of receipt of such commodities by Carrier in apparent good order and condition or as may be otherwise noted on the face of such form. In the event that a bill of lading is issued for any shipment its

payments to Carrier relating to the shipment and void all rate quotes.

In the event that the Broker's name is inserted in a bill of lading or any other shipping documentation, such insertion shall not change Broker's status as a property broker or Carrier's status as a motor carrier.

Upon acceptance of the shipment, Carrier shall assume liability for the cargo until proper delivery is made to the consignee. Carrier will obtain a delivery receipt signed by the consignee at the time of delivery showing the kind, quantity and condition of the commodity delivered at the specified destination and the time of delivery. Absence or loss of any such documents will not relieve the Carrier of responsibility for freight accepted by it. In the event any term or provision contained in such documents conflict in any way with any term or provision of this Agreement, the terms and provisions of this Agreement will take precedence and control.

6. <u>No Substituted Services and Diversion/Reconsignment</u> - Effective upon acceptance of a shipment from Broker for the Broker's customer's account, Carrier shall perform the transportation services itself and shall not re-broker, co-broker, assign, interline, subcontract or transfer the transportation of the shipment to another entity (collectively, "Substituted Services"). If Substituted Services of any type are used once Carrier has accepted the tender of the shipment from the Broker, any provision in this Agreement related to a limitation of liability for cargo damage, shortage/loss or delay shall be void and Carrier (i) will be liable to Broker's customer for any loss, damage or delay to Broker's customer's goods incurred during transportation services based on the "actual loss" as defined in Section 9 below and (ii) shall indemnify Broker as to any such loss, damage, or delay on the same basis. Carrier shall not have any right to, in any way, negate, eliminate, circumvent or alleviate Carrier's liability to Broker or Broker's customer which may be inconsistent with the provisions of this Agreement. Carrier will not allow the diversion or reconsignment of any shipment except upon written instructions by Broker or Broker's customer. Carrier will not accept instructions for diversion or reconsignment of any consignee or third party without the written consent of Broker or Broker's customer.

7. <u>Rates</u> - Carrier agrees to transport shipments tendered by Broker at the rates and charges as set forth in Broker's "Load and Rate Confirmation," which shall be signed by Carrier and transmitted by Carrier to Broker by facsimile (or other electronic means), for each shipment accepted by Carrier under this Agreement. Carrier and Broker agree that any tariff rates, accessorial charges, rules and regulations established and/or published by Carrier shall not apply to any shipment tendered under this Agreement unless specifically agreed to by Carrier and Broker, in writing. Any change in rates, charges, or rules and regulations shall be mutually agreed to and confirmed in writing, signed by both parties.

Rate Confirmation Sheets shall be deemed to be accepted amendments to this Agreement. Due to document storage considerations, the Rate Confirmation Sheet need not be attached to the original Agreement, but may be kept with the shipping papers that are retained as to the individual shipment. The same requirements of retention and availability to inspection that apply to the written agreement shall apply to the Rate Confirmation Sheet. If either party disputes the accuracy of the amended rate, that party shall, within 24 hours of receipt of it, notify the other party, and a disputed rate shall not become an amended rate until agreed to by both parties.

8. <u>Payment</u> - Carrier authorizes Broker to invoice Broker's customers for services provided by Carrier. Carrier agrees to invoice Broker, and only Broker, and acknowledges that Broker is the sole party responsible for payment of its invoices and assigns Broker all its rights to collect freight charges from Broker's customer or any responsible third party upon receipt of payment of its freight charges from Broker. Under no circumstance, shall Carrier seek payment from Broker's customers, the consignor, any

Broker agrees to pay Carrier for the transportation of shipments under this Agreement in accordance with the rates described herein, within thirty (30) days of receipt of Carrier's invoice and signed delivery document covering such transportation; provided, however in the event a shipment is the subject of cargo shortage/loss, damage or delay Broker reserves the right to withhold payment to Carrier for the shipment in question until the cargo shortage/loss, damage, or delay issue is resolved with Broker's customer. Broker reserves the right to deduct an amount equal to the shortage/loss, damage/spoilage, or delay claim resulting from the negligence or alleged negligence on the part of the Carrier, its agents, servants, or employees. Broker shall furnish to Carrier a written explanation and itemization of all deductions computed at the time deductions are made. Further, compensation paid under this Agreement may be withheld, in whole or in part, by Broker to satisfy any obligation paid by Broker which is the financial responsibility of Carrier.

9. Cargo Loss, Damage, and Delay

(a) Carrier shall be liable to Broker and Broker's customers, for the actual loss of, damage to, or delay of Broker's customers' freight, while under the Carrier's care, custody, or control according to the provisions of 49 U.S.C. Section 14706. The term "actual loss" shall mean the full invoice price charged by Broker's customer to its customers for the kind and quantity of product lost, damaged or destroyed, plus freight charges (unless included in the invoice price), less salvage value, if any, subject to a limitation of liability set forth in Appendix 1, unless otherwise agreed upon between Broker and Carrier in writing.

The liability of Carrier for delay in delivering a shipment shall be the greater of either the full actual value of the cargo or those damages that are reasonably foreseeable. No limitation of liability will apply as to delay. Carrier will have no lien or will accordingly waive its right to any lien upon any shipment of Shipper's cargo or portion thereof.

(b) Except as set forth below in this Subsection (b), Carrier agrees that the provisions contained in 49 CFR Part 370, shall govern the processing of claims for loss, damage, or delay to property and the processing of salvage.

(i) Carrier shall immediately notify Broker of any cargo damage, shortage/loss, or delay. Failure to comply with this notice provision shall void any limitation of liability and cause Carrier to be responsible for full liability of any damages or shortages of a shipment based on the "actual loss" as defined in Section 9(a) above without regard to Broker's customer's ability to mitigate damages.

(ii) The determination regarding the acceptability and/or salvageability of any food product intended for human consumption transported by Carrier shall be within the sole discretion of Broker's customer and shall be binding on Carrier;

(iii) The determination regarding the salvageability of any damaged cargo (other than food products) shall be determined by Broker's customer and Carrier shall be liable for all costs and expenses associated with Broker's customer's mitigation of damages including any inspection; storage;[5] preparation of the cargo for reshipping; and the reshipping, if applicable.

(iv) Claims based on concealed loss/damage reported to Carrier by Broker within five (5)

(v) It is the obligation of Carrier to properly inspect cargo upon the discovery of damage. In the event Carrier fails to inspect the cargo within five (5) business days of the date Carrier becomes aware of the damage, or upon receipt of the goods to be returned to the consignor because of the damage, whichever is earlier, Carrier waives its rights to inspect the goods and agrees to be bound by the fact presented by claimant.

(vi) Carrier shall not sell, or attempt to sell, Broker's customer's freight for salvage or otherwise without Broker's customer's prior written authorization. For any damaged product which Broker's customer permits Carrier to resell, Broker's customer will have the right to remove all identifying marks and labels on such product.

(vii) If the cargo is able to be repaired and restored to good marketable condition, Carrier will be liable for the costs of repairs including the costs of all labor and other necessary expenses, not to exceed the actual value of the kind and quality of product damage.

(viii) Failure of Carrier to pay, decline or offer settlement within thirty (30) days of receipt of the claim shall be deemed an admission by Carrier of full liability of the amount claimed and a material breach of this Agreement.

10. Term - The term of this Agreement shall be for a period of one (1) year from the Effective Date set forth above and shall automatically renew for additional one (1) year periods, unless terminated pursuant to Section 11 below.

11. Termination - If either party refuses or fails to perform any duty or obligation under this Agreement, fails to comply with applicable laws or regulations, suffers impairment of its financial responsibility, or otherwise defaults in any way, the non-defaulting party will have the option, without prejudice to any other right or remedy, to terminate this Agreement upon three (3) business days' advance written notice. Otherwise, either party may terminate this Agreement at any time without cause, by giving thirty (30) days prior written notice to the other party.

12. Insurance - Carrier shall procure and maintain at all times during the term of this Agreement, at its sole cost and expense, with reputable and financially responsible insurance carriers the following insurance coverages in not less than the amount specified below. Such amounts merely suggest minimum coverages and are not intended to establish any limitations of Carrier's liability for its acts or omissions. Additionally, the exclusions that may be contained in any of Carrier's insurance policies shall not exonerate Carrier from liability.

(a) Commercial Auto Liability Insurance insuring against liability for injury to persons, including injuries resulting in death, environmental restoration and loss or destruction of or physical damage to property, including any vehicle or other equipment furnished by the shipper for and in connection with the transportation services the Carrier renders, in a combined single limit of not less than $1,000,000.00 per occurrence;

(b) Cargo Insurance insuring Carrier against liability for loss or damage to commodities while in the custody, possession or control of Carrier in an amount not less than $100,000.00 per shipment which policy shall not contain any exclusions for negligent acts, infidelity, fraud, dishonesty, or criminal acts of Carrier's employees, agents, contractors, officers or directors; and

(c) Workers' compensation insurance for Carrier's employees in accordance with statutory requirements for all applicable jurisdictions.

13. <u>Indemnification</u> - Carrier shall defend, indemnify and hold harmless Broker and Broker's customers, their respective officers, directors, employees, agents, representatives, vendors and customers against any and all claims, demands, actions, causes of action and/or liabilities (actual, potential, threatened or pending) judgments, fines, penalties, orders, decrees, awards, costs, expenses, including attorneys' fees, settlements and claims on account of:

    (a) Loss or damage to property (other than cargo), or personal injury, including death, which may be sustained by the parties, their employees or third parties, arising out of or in connection with Carrier's performance of the services set forth herein;

    (b) Loss, damage or delay in transit as to all goods which Carrier receives through Broker for transport according to Rate Confirmation Sheet, until Carrier delivers such goods and the same are signed for by the consignee;

    (c) Carrier's breach of any of its representations, warranties and/or covenants in this Agreement; and

    (d) Carrier's failure to comply with workers' compensation requirements or any claim for workers' compensation asserted against Broker or its customer by Carrier's employees, or their personal representatives.

This provision will not be construed in any circumstance to constitute an indemnification contrary to any government law that prohibits indemnification against loss, liability, cost or expenses incident thereto, caused by the negligence of such indemnity. Exclusions in Carrier's insurance coverage(s) shall not exonerate Carrier from this liability.

14. <u>Confidentiality</u> - As part of the business relationship between Broker and Carrier, either party may be in or come into possession of information or data which constitutes trade secrets, know-how, confidential information, marketing plans, pricing, or anything else otherwise considered proprietary or secret by the other ("Confidential Information"). In consideration of the receipt of such Confidential Information and potential business, each party agrees to protect and maintain such Confidential Information in the utmost confidence, to use such Confidential Information solely in connection with their

business relationship, and to take all measures reasonably necessary to protect the Confidential Information.

Carrier agrees that Broker's charges to its customers are confidential and need not be disclosed to Carrier. Carrier specifically waives any rights it may have under 49 CFR § 371.3. Except as may be required by law, the terms and conditions of the Agreement and information pertaining to any Services will not be disclosed by either party to any other persons or entities, except to the directors, officers, employees, authorized contractors, attorneys, and accountants of each party. This mutual obligation of confidentiality will remain in effect during the terms of the Agreement and for a period of two years following any termination.

15. <u>Non-Solicitation</u> - Carrier agrees that during the term of this Agreement and for a period of _one_ (_1_) years from the date of termination of this Agreement, that neither Carrier nor any employee, officer, director, agent or otherwise of Carrier, shall directly or indirectly solicit traffic from any Broker, consignor, consignee, or customer of the Broker where (a) the availability of such shipments first became known to Carrier as a result of Broker's efforts; or (b) the shipments of the consignor, consignee, or customer of the Broker was first tendered to the Carrier by the Broker.

traffic first begins to move, to a commission from the Carrier of _fifteen_ percent (_15_%) of the transportation or revenue received on the movement of traffic. Carrier understands and agrees that the provisions of the aforementioned covenant not to compete are reasonable as to scope, duration, and geographic area, in light of the mutual promises and other valuable consideration the parties have agreed to in this Agreement. Further, Carrier agrees that any violation of the covenant not to compete will cause irreparable injury to Broker, and that Broker will be entitled to a restraining order and an injunction to stop the back-solicitation of traffic.

16. <u>Dispute Resolution</u> – Except as set forth in subsections (d)(i) and (d)(ii) below, any claim, dispute or controversy including, but not limited to, the interpretation of any federal statutory or regulatory provisions purported to gain compass by this Agreement; or enforcement of any statutory rights emanating or relating to this Agreement shall be resolved on an individual basis (and not as part of a class action) exclusively between Broker and Carrier.

The proceedings will be conducted under the rules of (select one): ___Transportation Arbitration and Mediation PLLC ("TAM"); ___ American Arbitration Association ("AAA"); or ___ Transportation ADR Council, Inc. ("ADR"), upon mutual agreement of the Parties, or if no agreement, then at Broker's sole discretion. The Parties may however agree between themselves that the arbitration proceedings may be conducted outside of the administrative control of the TAM, AAA or ADR. Any arbitration proceedings under this Agreement shall be governed by the following rules:

(a) A written demand for arbitration must be mailed to the other Party within _eighteen_ (_18__) months of the occurrence of the claim breach other than giving rise to the controversy or claim. **Failure to make such timely demand for arbitration shall constitute an absolute bar to the institution of any proceedings and a waiver of any claim.** The demand for arbitration shall identify the provision(s) of this Agreement alleged to have been breached and shall state the issue to be submitted to arbitration and the remedy sought. The demand for arbitration will be forwarded to the arbitration service selected through agreement of the Parties, as outlined above, or as selected by Broker and the proceedings shall be conducted at the office of TAM, AAA or ADR nearest Cleveland, Ohio or such other place as mutually agreed upon in writing. The arbitration may be conducted by conference call or video conferencing upon agreement of the Parties, or as directed by the acting arbitration association. The decision of the arbitrator(s) shall be binding and final and the award for the arbitrator may be entered as judgment in any court of competent jurisdiction. A rational and reasoning of the decision of the arbitrative(s) shall be fully explained in a written opinion.

(b) As to any dispute or controversy which under the terms of this Agreement is a proper subject of arbitration, no suited law or in equity based on such dispute or controversy shall be instituted by either party other than a suit to conform, enforce, vacate, modify or correct the award of the arbitrator(s) as provided by law; provided, however, that this clause shall not limit Broker's right to obtain any provision or remedy including, without limitation, injunctive relief, writ for recovery of possession or similar relief from any court of competent jurisdiction, as may be necessary and Broker's sole judgment to protect its rights.

(c) General pleadings and discovery processes related to the arbitration proceeding shall

(d) This arbitration provision is subject to the two exceptions set forth below.

(i) (BROKER INITIAL____; CARRIER INITIAL____.) Subject to the time limitation set forth above, for disputes where the amount in controversy exceeds $3,000, Broker shall have the right, but not the obligation, to select litigation in order to resolve any disputes arising hereunder. In the event of litigation the prevailing Party shall be entitled to recover costs, expenses and reasonable attorney fees, including but not limited to any incurred on appeals.

(ii) (BROKER INITIAL____; CARRIER INITIAL____.) Subject to the time limitation set forth above, for disputes where the amount in controversy does not exceed $3,000, Broker shall have the right, but not the obligation, to select litigation in small claims court order to resolve any disputes arising hereunder. The prevailing Party shall be entitled to recover costs, expenses and reasonable attorney fees, including but not limited to any incurred on appeals.

(iii) Venue, controlling law, and jurisdiction in any legal proceedings under Subparagraphs (i) or (ii) above shall be in Cuyahoga County, Ohio.

17. Force Majeure - The obligation of Carrier to furnish and of Broker to use the Services provided for in this Agreement will be suspended temporarily during the period in which either party is prevented from performing due to fire, flood, strikes, lockout, epidemic, accident, regulatory action or other causes beyond its reasonable control. The party experiencing force majeure will notify the other party promptly and take all reasonable steps to eliminate the interruption and resume normal operations as soon as possible.

8

18. Waiver/Enforceability - The waiver of a breach of any term or condition of this Agreement will not constitute the waiver of any other breach of the same or any other term. To be enforceable, a waiver must be in writing signed by a duly authorized representative of the waiving Party. The unenforceability of a provision of this Agreement or portion thereof will not affect the enforceability of any other provision of this Agreement or portion thereof.

19. Entire Agreement - This Agreement, together with any Appendices hereto, constitutes the entire agreement between the parties with respect to the subject matter hereof, and supersedes all prior oral or written representations and agreements.

20. Governing Law - This Agreement is to be construed according to federal law governing transportation and the laws of the State of Ohio and the parties hereby stipulate the exclusive jurisdiction of the courts situated in Cuyahoga County, Ohio, or the Federal Court for the Northern District of Ohio, Eastern Division. If any part of this Agreement is determined to be contrary to law, such determination shall not affect the validity of any other terms or conditions. Carrier shall pay all costs, expenses and attorney fees which may be expended or incurred by Broker or Broker's customer in successfully enforcing this Agreement or any provision thereof, or in exercising any right or remedy of Broker or its customers against Carrier, or in any arbitration or litigation incurred by Broker because of any act or omission of Carrier under this Agreement.

55

21. Notices - Unless otherwise provided, notices required under this Agreement must be in writing and delivered by (i) registered or certified U.S. Mail, return receipt requested, (ii) hand delivered, (iii)

and if not received, then the date the follow-up copy is received. Notices must be delivered to the following addresses or at such other addresses as may be later designated by notice:

        To Carrier:

        Attn:
        Facsimile:

        To Broker: Example Logistics LLC
        00000 Sample Road.
        Anywhere, US 00000
        Attn:
        Facsimile:

22. <u>Counterparts</u> - This Agreement may be executed in one or more counterparts, each of which is an original but all of which together will constitute one and the same agreement.

9

IN WITNESS WHEREOF, this Agreement is executed by authorized representatives of the parties, effective as of the date set forth above.

CARRIER BROKER

Signature Signature

Printed Name: Printed Name: Brian Ferancy_ Title: Title: V.P., Sales & Business Development

10

APPENDIX 1

Limitations of Liability

Absent a written agreement between Broker and Carrier to the contrary, the cargo liability of any Carrier contracted by Broker to transport Broker's customer's freight shall be subject to the following limitations:

    (a) $25.00 per pound, per package for less than truckload ("LTL") shipments (ground shipments up to 20,000 lbs.);

    (b) $100,000.00 per truckload shipment; or

    (c) $100.00 per package for shipments if a parcel carrier unless a higher value is declared at the time of tender and a greater charge paid as provided in the parcel carrier's general rules tariff.

EXAMPLE LOGISTICS

Dear Carrier Partner,

Example Logistics currently offers a variety of quick payment options, available for a minimal discount. Please take a moment to complete our **Quick Payment Options Agreement,** and we will provide payment remitted in two to 14 business days.[1]

To be eligible for Quick Pay, we must receive the following:

- **A completed Quick Pay agreement form for each invoice submitted.**
- **Your invoice for the contracted amount.**
- **Non-exception delivery documents signed by the consignee and driver.**

Please do not submit the Quick Pay form until you have all the required documents

Please contact the Example Logistics Accounting Services Department at 000-000-0000 (option 0) for more information.

Sincerely,

Mark Doe
Revenue Services
Example Logistics
00000 Sample Rd.
Anywhere, USA 00000
P: 000-000-0000 option 0
F: 000-000-0000
E: billing@examplelogistics.com
www.examplelogistics.com

---

[1] Required paperwork must be submitted by email to Example Logistics by 11:00AM EST to be processed for that day. Quick Pay via check is processed and paid Monday-Friday only, excluding holidays.

Example Logistics Quick Payment Options Agreement

This form represents an agreement between Example Logistics and _____ to pay the below referenced invoice according to the terms as selected on this form. By submitting this form, the undersigned acknowledges that this invoice has not been factored or sold to another party.

Requirements:
To be eligible for Quick Pay, we must receive with this form your invoice for the contracted amount along with non-exception delivery documents signed by the consignee and driver.
A completed Quick Payment Agreement Form must be submitted for <u>each invoice.</u>

Invoice Information:
Example Logistics Load #: _____
Invoice Amount: _____ (Contracted amount prior to Quick Pay Discount)

Select from the options below to sign-up for the Example Logistics Quick Payment program. After making your selection, please sign and email to billing@partnership.com

Quick Payment Options:

_____ **2 Business Days via T-Check (T-Check code not given to driver)** with a 3% discount upon receipt of invoice, rate confirmation, signed bills of lading and/or proof of delivery containing no exceptions. Please email legible copies of the required paperwork to PartnerShip at billing@examplelogistics.com (T-Check payments are charged additional $10.00 fee)

_____ **14 Day Payment – PAID VIA CHECK MAILED 14 DAYS AFTER RECEIPT OF REQUIRED PAPERWORK** – with a 1% discount upon receipt of invoice, rate confirmation, signed bills of lading and/or proof of delivery containing no exceptions. Please email legible copies of the required paperwork to PartnerShip at billing@examplelogistics.com

_____ **21 Day Payment – PAID VIA CHECK MAILED 21 DAYS AFTER RECEIPT OF REQUIRED PAPERWORK** – no fee

PartnerShip LLC will honor your quick pay for all invoices submitted in good standing until written notice to cancel this agreement is received by either party. This agreement will become an addendum to the "Broker Carrier" contract previously agreed to by the carrier and PartnerShip LLC. PartnerShip LLC may at any time make changes to this agreement for the conduct of its business, as it may, in its judgment, deem necessary or desirable. This agreement may be canceled at any time. Any such amendments or cancellations will be effective after notice of the amendments has been made to the participating parties.

_____
Company Name

_____
Company Address & Phone

MC #

DISPATCHING YOUR TRUCK

You should always provide the broker with email updates about:

1. ETA to shipper
2. Check in at shipper
3. Loaded at shipper (check-out time) and ETA to receiver
4. Check in time at receiver
5. Unload and check-out time at the receiver

You should always provide the broker with the POD (signed BOLs) as soon as they become available.

DISPATCH SCHEDULE

Sunday
Carrier:_____
Load#:_____
Pickup#_____
Time:_____
Location:_____
Truck#____ Trailer#____

Notes:

Monday
Load#:_____
Pickup#_____
Time:_____
Location:_____
Truck#____ Trailer#____

Notes:

Tuesday
Load#:_____
Pickup#_____
Time:_____
Location:_____
Truck#____ Trailer#____

Notes:

Wednesday
Load#:_____
Pickup#_____
Time:_____
Location:_____
Truck#____ Trailer#____

Notes:

THURSDAY
Load#:_____
Time:_____
Location:_____
Truck#____ Trailer#____

Notes:

FRIDAY
Load#:_____
Time:_____
Location:_____
Truck#____ Trailer#____

Notes:

SATURDAY
Load#:_____
Time:_____
Location:_____
Truck#____ Trailer#____

Notes:

Equip. Type
_____

miles/gallon
_____

Natl. Truck Average
_____

MC#_____

DOT#_____

PHONE#_____

EMAIL ADDRESS:_____

INSURANCE #_____ LAST 6 OF VIN#_____

PROCESSING PAPERWORK FOR PAYMENT

Once a load is completed, the motor carrier should send you scanned pdf copies of the Proof of Delivery (POD). You should email the scanned copies to the broker listed on the rate confirmation. Make sure the copies are clear! Illegible copies hold up payments. Your email should look something like this:

Subject: (load number) POD

Body: Please see attached POD for load #

Thank you
Company name
MC#

You should send an invoice, rate confirmation, POD along with any receipts to the email payment address listed on the rate confirmation. Always cc the motor carrier's email address so that they know the paperwork has been submitted. EVERY LOAD COMPLETED SHOULD INCLUDE CLEAR PDF COPIES OF AN INVOICE, RATE CONFIRMATION, SIGNED BILL OF LADINGS (BOLS) AND RECEIPTS (if applicable). Once paperwork has been submitted, you can record on your calendar the expected day the account should be credited. If you are an independent carrier, you should keep a file of all POD for your records in a file folder. Be sure to include the word "QUICKPAY" OR THE NAME OF THE FACTORING COMPANY on the invoice!

Sample Invoice

MOTOR CARRIER'S NAME ADDRESS CITY, STATE		INVOICE
PHONE: Email address		INVOICE Date:

| Bill To | BROKERS COMPANY NAME
ADDRESS
CITY, STATE

BOOKING CONTACT:
PHONE:
LOAD #:
RATE: | SHIPPER:
CITY, STATE, ZIP

RECEIVER:
CITY, STATE, ZIP |

HOW YOU WANT TO BE PAID (IE QUICKPAY OR FACTORING)

DELIVERY DATE	DESCRIPTION APPOINTMENT TIME	UNIT PRICE	LINE TOTAL
	RATE:		$
	FUEL ADVANCES:		$
	LUMPER:		$
		TOTAL	$

THANK YOU FOR YOUR BUSINESS!

* Electronically signed

sample

Carrier Confirmation

Page 1

Carrier Mgr: ▓

Order# ▓

Carrier:	▓	Contact:	▓
		Phone:	
Date:	▓	Fax:	
Driver:	▓ Trailer: ▓	Driver cell:	▓

Order	Order: ▓	Commodity: ▓
	Miles: ▓	Weight: ▓
	Temp:	Trailer: ▓
	PO# ▓	Reference:

PU 1 — pickup information
- Name: ▓
- Address: ▓
- Phone:
- Reference number: ▓
- Date: ▓ 1400
- Contact: ▓

SO 2 — delivery information
- Name: ▓
- Address: ▓
- Phone:
- Reference number: PO ▓
- Date: ▓ 0700
- Contact: Main ▓

Payment
- Carrier Freight Pay: ▓
- Total Carrier Pay: ▓ ← rate

Carrier Instructions and Requirements: This form must be completed and returned before driver can be loaded.
▓: **TAKE SPECIAL NOTE: DELIVERY CONDITION REPORT MUST BE SUBMITTED WITH PODs for payment**
Any over, short or damage MUST be reported to ▓ Dispatcher AT time of delivery.

At RECEIVER: NO LUMPER charges & NO product to be put back on trailer.

Please Sign: ▓
(X) Accept
( ) Decline

Driver Name: ▓
Driver Cell: ▓
Driver Email: ▓
Tractor #: ▓
Trailer #: ▓

Attention: ▓

PAYMENT STATUS CHECK

After you have submitted your documents for payment, record on your calendar the date the payment should credit the motor carrier's account. If the account is not credited on the expected date, you can send an email to the accounting department for a payment status update. Sometimes a payment inquiry email address is listed on the rate confirmation. Be sure to include the load number followed by payment status. If you need to make a phone call, ask to speak with the accounting department.

Subject: Load #12345 payment status

Body: I would like the payment status for load # 12345

Thank you
Company Name
MC#

HOW TO FILE A CLAIM AGAINST A BOND

The purpose of the surety bond is to make sure the motor carrier receives payment on a load that has been delivered. A broker should always pay the motor carrier for a service that has been provided. If you have made several attempts to receive payment on a load, and you feel like the broker is giving you the "runaround" for payment, your next step is to file a claim. You can file a claim by contacting the broker's bond company (which should have been provided in the initial setup packet). If a bond was not included in the packet, load boards like DAT have a tool where you can view a broker's bond information.

It is very important when you initially set up with a broker to look for their bond information, Broker Authority, and credit references in the new carrier setup packet. Always keep this information on file in case you have to file a claim.

On the DAT load board you can click on tools under the DAT dashboard and select "DAT directory". At the top left corner of the next page, enter the broker's MC#. Scroll down to the bond section to locate the bond information. The name of the bond company should be listed. You will need the policy number which should be listed. Sometimes there is a phone number or email address. Sometimes you might have to do a google search of the bond company to get a phone number.

You can call the bond company and listen to the prompts and select the option regarding surety bonds. Explain who you are, and how you would like to file a claim against a broker for unpaid invoice(s). You will have to provide the policy number, your email address, and other information to get the process started. The bond company should provide you with an email address where you can submit supporting documents such as the invoice, rate confirmation, signed BOLS, and any receipts along with any email correspondence you have made to the broker regarding payment status.

The bond company will review the claim and issue you a claim number. The bond company will reach out to the broker and allow them to respond to the claim. When you file the claim, it doesn't mean you will get your money right away. The bond company will give the broker time to respond to the claim. If you have proof documenting you provided the service, the broker will pay before the bond company issues a payment because a claim against the bond could result in possible fees, higher premiums upon renewal, or loss of bond for the broker.

Setup Requirements

To set up as a carrier with a broker the following information is needed.

    Carrier Contract- Provided by the broker (usually sent to you by email.)
- Operating Authority
- Certificate of Insurance
- W-9 (for tax purposes) Tax ID #_____(never put down your social security#)
- Email address (brokers send rate sheets to your email)_____
- Voided check (for direct deposit)
- Truck #_____Year_____miles per gallon_____
- Trailer #_____Year_____
- Photo ID (sometimes they may ask for a Driver's License)
- Notice of Assignment if you factor your loads.
- Photo of equipment with visible company name and MC#
- SCAC number (if applicable)
- Tanker endorsed Y or N
- TWIC card Y or N twic #_____
- Hazardous material Y or N
- Smartway Carrier Y or N

The setup process usually takes about 15 minutes. A rate sheet will be sent to the email address you provided. The rate sheet will tell you how much you will make off the load. Once the load is completed submit the rate sheet, along with an invoice, all Bill of Ladings (BOL's), and lumper receipts. Some brokers will allow you to submit copies of everything to a quickpay email address while others want paperwork submitted to TRANSFLO. Some brokers will want original paperwork and do not accept copies. Some brokers pay by comcheck, ACH quickpay. The fees the brokers charge can vary from 1.5% to 5%.

My payment information
Name:_____Bank Name & Account #_____
Phone:_____(zelle, cash app)_____
EIN#:_____

DISPATCHING AGREEMENT

This agreement is entered on_____20____between _____

MC#_____and_____EIN # _____

I agree to allow_____to NEGOTIATE RATES ON MY BEHALF TO INCLUDE THE FOLLOWING: COMPLETE BROKER CARRIER PACKETS, REQUEST CERTIFICATE OF INSURANCE, PROVIDE BROKER WITH OPERATING AUTHORITY, W-9, AND OTHER SUPPORTING DOCUMENTS, RUN CREDIT CHECKS, AND CHECK CALLS FOR A WEEKLY FEE IN THE AMOUNT OF_____% OF THE RATE.

☐ I agree to allow_____to use my signature only as it pertains to new carrier

setup packets and rate confirmations. _____
            Initial here

☐ I agree to allow_____to request fuel advances on my behalf.

        _____
        Initial here

I agree to allow_____to PROCESS INVOICE FOR PAYMENT WHICH INCLUDES SUBMITTING INVOICE, RATE CONFIRMATION, BOL'S & ANY ACCESSORIAL DOCUMENTS TO RECEIVE PAYMENT ON A LOAD, AND PAYMENT STATUS CHECKS FOR A WEEKLY FEE IN THE AMOUNT OF $___.

_____   _____
Motor Carrier Signature   Dispatcher Signature

SAMPLE DISPATCHING SCRIPT

If there is a reference # posted on the load board

Hi, this is (your name) with (motor carriers company name). I am calling about reference #

If there is no reference # posted

Hi, this is (your name) with (motor carriers company name). I am calling about the (origin city state) to (destination city state) picking up (date)

Yes, I do have that one available. Can I get your MC#?

MC#

This is a 1 and 1 pick today out of Atlanta, Georgia at 10 am, delivers next day to Asheboro NC at 8 am. It's a truck load of non hazardous cleaning products weighing at 8,869 lbs. 325 loaded miles. Rate is $800 dollars. (or what kind of rate do you need?)

You should be listening and writing the information down. This is when you can start to negotiate your rate based on the research you have done about your particular lane.

****Always ask about the details of the load before you talk about the rate!

Is (posted rate) the best you can do on that? (or what is the average for this lane?) You should know your rate before you call.

TRUCKING GLOSSARY

Load Board - a software that contains information about freight that needs to be picked up and delivered across the United States.

Independent motor carrier - the employer and driver of a commercial vehicle Book a load- a term dispatchers use to say I want to transport this product Freight-goods transported in bulk by truck, train, aircraft, or ship.

Shipper - a person or company that has freight that needs to be transported.

Receiver - a person or company that needs freight from a Shipper.

Consignee - a person or business who is financially responsible for the receipt of a shipment.

Motor Carrier - a person or company that is federally licensed and/or bonded to transport freight with their equipment.

Lane - Transportation routes from point A to B that carriers can run regularly.

Deadhead - the number of empty miles a truck has to drive to its next pickup.

Invoice - a bill.

Bill of Lading (BOL) - a document that contains information about the freight which includes product, weight, amount, and any identifying information about the freight.

POD (proof of delivery) - a document signed or stamped by the receiver (consignee) proving the product was delivered; a signed BOL

FTL - full truck load.

LTL - less than full truck load.

Pickup number - a special number provided by the broker. A carrier must provide to a shipper to get freight loaded onto the carrier's equipment.

Operating Authority - a motor carrier's legal right to operate a commercial motor vehicle in the United States.

Rate confirmation - a legally binding contract between a broker and carrier with information about a load that needs to be transported.

TONU - truck ordered not used. When a shipper orders a truck to pick up but cancels after the truck has been dispatched. The amount paid to the truck can range from $150-$300.

Carrier setup packet - documentation that verifies a carrier can legally transport goods across state lines.

MC# - a federally regulated number that is assigned to a carrier that authorizes the legal transportation of freight across state lines.

DOT# - a number issued by the Department of Transportation that tracks safety information about a Motor Carrier.

Factoring Company - a company that buys another company's accounts receivables.

Truck ordered not used (TONU) - a fee a motor carrier can charge to the broker when a contract has been canceled at the request of the broker. The amount can range from $150-$250 depending on the broker.

Layover - when a driver is delayed by a shipper or receiver by at least one day. Layover varies by broker.

Quickpay - a payment option to receive monies more quickly.

Lumper - a reimbursable fee to unload a truck, usually paid by the broker.

Comcheck - a form of payment.

Detention - a period of time that is paid to the on time truck usually 2 hours after the scheduled appointment.

Accounts Receivables - money due to a company once a service is provided.

Notice of Assignment - a legal document that allows a factoring company to issue payment to a carrier once proof of delivery, invoice, rate confirmation, lumpers, advances, and any applicable fees are submitted. The motor carrier pays a small fee to the factoring company to receive money within 24-48 hours.

Certificate of Insurance (COI) - a document issued by an insurance company that verifies the existence of an insurance policy in the motor carrier's business name.

EIN# - a unique nine digit number assigned by the IRS to business entities in the United States for the purpose of identification.

W-9 - an IRS form that is filled out by self-employed workers for companies they are providing services.

www.ingramcontent.com/pod-product-compliance
Lightning Source LLC
Chambersburg PA
CBHW061758290426
44109CB00030B/2890